Baby Pets

Bobbie Kalman

✿ Crabtree Publishing Company

www.crabtreebooks.com

Created by Bobbie Kalman

Dedicated by Andrea Crabtree
To the coolest kids I know!
Jake, Travis, Charlie, Hailey, and Nicole

**Author and
Editor-in-Chief**
Bobbie Kalman

Editors
Kathy Middleton
Crystal Sikkens

Photo research
Bobbie Kalman

Design
Bobbie Kalman
Katherine Berti
Samantha Crabtree
(logo and front cover)

Print and production coordinator
Katherine Berti

Prepress technician
Katherine Berti

Special thanks to
Brooke Boudreau, Sarah Chan, Alissa Lefebvre,
and Keith Makubuya

Illustrations
Bonna Rouse: page 6

Photographs
Comstock: pages 15 (bottom left), 18 (carrots and broccoli)
Marc Crabtree: pages 13 (litter), 15 (top), 17 (top right and
top and bottom left), 21, 22 (leash and collar), 23 (all
except middle right and bottom right)
Photodisc: page 18 (cucumber)
All other images by Shutterstock

Library and Archives Canada Cataloguing in Publication

Kalman, Bobbie
    Baby pets / Bobbie Kalman.

(It's fun to learn about baby animals)
Includes index.
Issued also in electronic format.
ISBN 978-0-7787-4075-9 (bound).--ISBN 978-0-7787-4080-3 (pbk.)

    1. Pets--Juvenile literature. 2. Animals--Infancy--Juvenile literature.
I. Title. II. Series: It's fun to learn about baby animals

SF416.2.K33 2012   j636.088'7   C2011-907666-7

Library of Congress Cataloging-in-Publication Data

Kalman, Bobbie.
 Baby pets / Bobbie Kalman.
    p. cm. -- (It's fun to learn about baby animals)
 Includes index.
 ISBN 978-0-7787-4075-9 (reinforced library binding : alk. paper) -- ISBN 978-
0-7787-4080-3 (pbk. : alk. paper) -- ISBN 978-1-4271-7887-9 (electronic pdf) --
ISBN 978-1-4271-8002-5 (electronic html)
 1. Domestic animals--Infancy--Juvenile literature. 2. Pets--Infancy--Juvenile
literature. I. Title.

 SF75.5.K348 2012
 636'.07--dc23
                                          2011046087

Crabtree Publishing Company

Printed in Canada/012012/MA20111130

www.crabtreebooks.com   1-800-387-7650

Published in Canada
Crabtree Publishing
616 Welland Ave.
St. Catharines, Ontario
L2M 5V6

Published in the United States
Crabtree Publishing
PMB 59051
350 Fifth Avenue, 59th Floor
New York, New York 10118

Published in the United Kingdom
Crabtree Publishing
Maritime House
Basin Road North, Hove
BN41 1WR

Published in Australia
Crabtree Publishing
3 Charles Street
Coburg North
VIC 3058

What is in this book?

Baby pets

Baby pets are young animals that live with people. Do you have a pet? What is it called? Most baby animals are called by different names than the names of adult animals. What are the baby pets on these pages called?

*A baby dog is called a **pup** or **puppy**.*

A baby cat is called a **kitten**.

Baby chinchillas are called **kits**.

A baby rabbit is a kitten or **bunny**.

guinea pig mother and pup

Baby guinea pigs, gerbils, and hamsters are all called pups.

gerbil pup

hamster pups

A baby pony is called a **foal**.

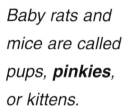

Baby rats and mice are called pups, **pinkies**, or kittens.

rat mother and pinkie

Mammal bodies

All the baby pets in this book are **mammals**. Mammals are animals with **backbones**. A backbone is a group of bones in the middle of an animal's back. Most mammals also have fur or hair on their bodies. Mammals are **warm-blooded** animals. The body temperatures of warm-blooded animals always stay about the same. It does not matter if they are in warm or cold places.

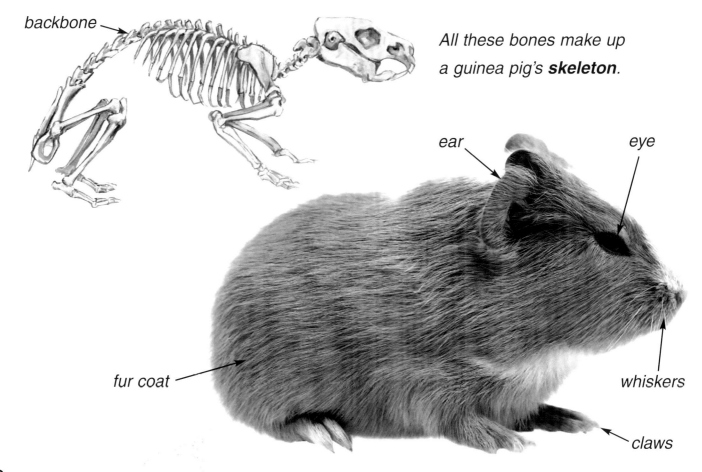

backbone

All these bones make up a guinea pig's **skeleton**.

ear

eye

fur coat

whiskers

claws

Mammals are born

Mammals do not **hatch** from eggs the way birds do. Mammal babies are **born** live. You are a mammal, and you were born, too. After mammal babies are born, their mothers feed them milk that is made inside their bodies. Drinking mother's milk is called **nursing**.

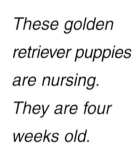

Birds hatch from eggs, but mammals are born.

These golden retriever puppies are nursing. They are four weeks old.

Time with Mom

Mammal babies need to stay with their mothers until they are **weaned**, or stop nursing. Different baby pets need to be with their mothers for different periods of time, until the mothers stop feeding them. Baby pets should never be taken away from their mothers too early!

Newborn kittens are tiny and helpless. They must stay with their mothers until they are eight weeks old.

Puppy dogs should stay with their mothers until they are eight to eleven weeks old.

Bunny rabbits need to stay with their mothers until they are at least six weeks old.

Gerbils, hamsters, rats, mice, guinea pigs, and chinchillas are animals called **rodents** (see pages 16–19). Guinea pigs and chinchillas are born with hair and are able to see and hear. Gerbils, hamsters, rats, and mice are born without hair and cannot see or hear at birth. Their hair grows in about a week after they are born, and they can hear and see after about two weeks. They need to stay with their mothers for about three to five weeks after they are born.

Baby chinchillas nurse for six to eight weeks. They stay with their mothers until they are weaned.

A mother rat is carrying a newborn pinkie.

Guinea pig mothers keep their pups warm while they sleep.

These newborn mice pinkies have no hair.

These week-old mice pinkies have grown some hair.

A mother pony feeds and protects its foal for at least one year.

This hamster pup is one week old. It is still blind, but it has hair.

9

Puppy dogs

Yorkshire terrier

Puppies are born in **litters**, or groups, of up to twelve babies. They are popular pets because they are cute, loyal, and fun. There are many kinds of puppies. Some grow to be huge dogs, and others stay very small. If you live in an apartment, a small dog will probably be a better pet for you. A puppy that will grow into a big dog will be happier in a house with a big yard or nearby park.

This golden retriever puppy will grow to be a large dog.

This white baby chihuahua puppy is almost the same size as its small moth

Puppies need to go for a walk at least once a day.

English bulldog puppy

cavalier King Charles spaniel

Until they are six months old, puppies need to be fed three to four times a day. They can eat dry food or canned food.

This boy is training his Alaskan Klee Kai puppy. Puppies need to be trained to follow orders.

New pet puppies should see a **veterinarian**, or doctor for animals. The vet will check the puppy for diseases and give it shots to keep it from getting sick in the future.

Pet Kittens

Kittens love to play.

Cats are smart, cute, and loving. They enjoy playing with people and can be very funny! Cats are also happy being on their own. They make good pets for people who must be away from home during the day.

Kitten care

Kittens depend on people for food and water. They also need love and attention. You will need an adult's help to care for your kitten.

Kittens need plenty of fresh water and milk to drink.

Kittens love climbing into containers like this old bucket. They seem to laugh a lot!

"What do we need?"

What do kittens need?

Below are a few things that your kitten will need. Others are shown on page 22.

Your kitten will need good food so it can grow. Buy food that is made for kittens.

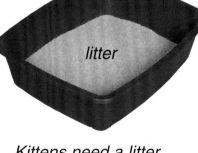

litter

Kittens need a litter box with clean litter.

The kitten on the left is being hugged by its mother. It will need lots of hugs from you after it leaves its mom.

13

Pet bunnies

Pet rabbits are related to **wild** rabbits. Wild rabbits do not live with people. They live in groups called **herds**. Wild rabbits dig underground homes called **warrens**, which have many **burrows**, or tunnels. Rabbits sleep in the burrows during the day. At night, they leave their warrens to gather food. Pet rabbits are also active mainly at night.

Like wild rabbits, pet bunnies also like living with other bunnies.

Rabbit food

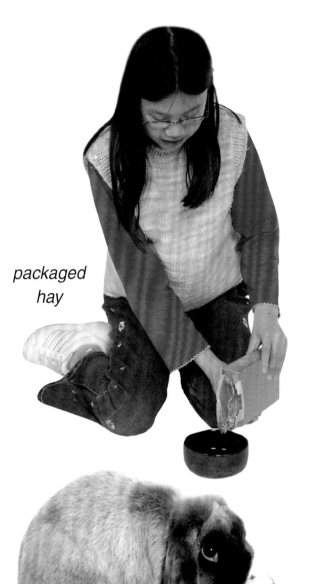

packaged hay

Bunnies drink their mothers' milk until they are seven weeks old. After that, they need plenty of grass hay every day. You can buy packaged hay for your bunny at a pet store. At twelve weeks, bunnies also need to eat fresh green vegetables. Some healthy vegetables are broccoli, celery leaves, lettuce, and baby greens. You can also feed adult rabbits fruits and vegetables, such as chopped apples, carrots, and pears.

apples and pears

green vegetables

carrots

15

Rodent babies

These gerbil babies were just born. They are pink, blind, and hairless. They are not yet ready to be pets.

Hamsters, gerbils, mice, and rats are mammals called rodents. Most rodent pets are small and have four sharp front teeth that never stop growing.

Big litters

The baby rodents on these pages are born in big litters. Their mothers look after them for the first three to five weeks. When the babies stop nursing, they are ready to be your pets.

Rat pinkies make great pets. They are very smart and friendly. They enjoy playing and snuggling with their owners, just as they do with one another.

Hamster pups are cute and fun to watch as they scamper around their cages. They are small, so they do not need much space.

Gerbil pups are very curious. They love to explore and try new toys. They climb, jump, and dig.

Mice pinkies are very intelligent pets. You might be surprised how friendly they can be—just ask this kitten!

You can help your rodent pet keep its teeth in good condition by giving it hard pieces of fruit-tree wood to **gnaw**, or chew on. Gnawing grinds down the teeth and keeps them from getting too long.

fruit-tree wood

Guinea pig pups

A guinea pig does not like to be alone. It should always have another guinea pig to live with after it leaves its mother.

Guinea pigs are relatives of **cavies**. Cavies are rodents that live in the mountains of South America. Guinea pig pups are covered in fur when they are born, and they can see and hear. Guinea pigs make great pets because they are cute, cuddly, and friendly. They love to spend time with people. These fun pets are full of energy and love to run and jump. They need large cages (see page 23).

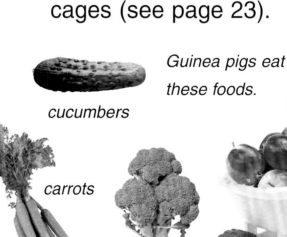

cucumbers

Guinea pigs eat these foods.

carrots

broccoli

apples

Chinchilla kits

Chinchillas are also rodents from South America. They are soft and furry pets that are the size of bunnies. They like to play in the evening. They need exercise to be happy and healthy. Chinchilla kits like to run outside their cage for at least one hour a day.

You must be very gentle while holding your pets. Never squeeze or drop them!

Chinchilla mothers have one to six kits.

19

Pony foals

Many children dream of having a pony as a pet. A pony is a small horse with a thick fur coat and short legs. It is a mammal. Ponies are beautiful, friendly animals. A foal, or baby pony, is born with all its fur. Just one day after it is born, a foal can play, swim, and even **gallop**, or run fast!

Needing its mother

A young foal, however, still needs to be with its mother for at least one year. The foal nurses for six months, but it also begins to eat solid foods when it is one month old. It eats grass, hay, and grains.

Pony foals need to be four years old before they are ready to carry riders.

Pony care

Caring for a pony is a lot of work! You will need to make sure your pony is fed, **groomed**, or cleaned, and exercised every day. Also, ponies cannot live in your home the way smaller pets can. They need a big place to live, such as a **stable**. A stable is a building where ponies and horses live and are fed.

*A pony's **stall**, or living area, in the stable needs to be large and airy. The pony needs to move around in the stall and lie down in it comfortably.*

You will need different brushes and combs for grooming a pony. You will also need a hoof pick to clean its hooves and a sponge to wipe its face. A salt lick gives the pony the salt its body needs.

sponge

brushes

comb

hoof pick

salt lick

21

What do pets need?

These two pages show some of the things you will need for your pets. Different pets need different things. What does your pet need?

*Kittens travel from place to place in a **carrier** like this one.*

leash

collar

Puppies need a leash and collar when they are taken for walks. The collar should have a tag with your phone number on it.

scoop

*Kittens like to scratch. A **scratching post** like this one will save your furniture from getting ripped by a kitten's claws.*

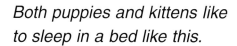

Both puppies and kittens like to sleep in a bed like this.

Kittens need a litter box. Bunnies and some rodent pets also use litter boxes.

sleeping box

hay

water bottle

Gunea pigs, bunnies, and chinchillas need large cages. They need water bottles and hay in the cages.

Puppies need to have a bath when they are dirty.

Hamsters, gerbils, rats, and mice like to hide in small houses. They love to play with toys, too.

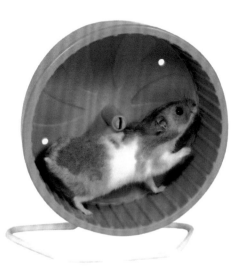

Pets are part of your family. They need to be hugged and loved.

Rodents also like to run inside wheels to get exercise.

Most pets with hair or fur need to be brushed.

23

Words to Know and Index

cats/kittens
pages 5, 8,
12–13, 17, 22

chinchillas/kits
pages 5, 9,
19, 23

dogs/puppies
pages 4, 7, 8,
10–11, 22

gerbils/pups
pages 5, 9,
16, 17, 23

**guinea pigs/
pups**
pages 5, 6,
9, 18, 23

hamsters/pups
pages 5, 9, 16,
17, 23

mice/pinkies
pages 5, 9,
16, 17, 23

Other index words
bodies pages 6, 7, 21
food pages 11, 12,
   13, 14, 15, 18, 20
fur/hair pages 6, 9, 16,
   18, 19, 20, 23
litters pages 10, 16
mammals pages 6, 7,
   8, 20
mothers pages 7, 8–9,
   10, 13, 15, 16, 18, 19, 2●
nursing pages 7, 8, 9,
   15, 16, 20
rodents pages 9, 16–17
   18, 19, 22, 23
skeleton page 6

ponies/foals
pages 5, 9,
20–21

rabbits/bunnies
pages 5, 8, 14–15,
19, 22, 23

rats/pinkies
pages 5, 9,
16, 23

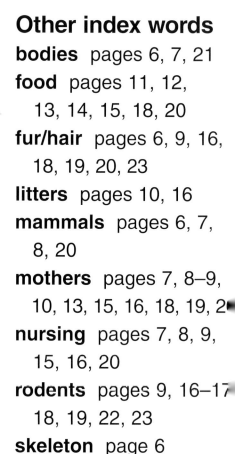